ANCIENT CULTURES AND CIVILIZATIONS

THE CULTURE OF
MONGOLS

Vic Kovacs

NEW YORK

Published in 2017 by **The Rosen Publishing Group, Inc.**
29 East 21st Street, New York, NY 10010

Cataloging-in-Publication Data
Names: Kovacs, Vic.
Title: The culture of the Mongols / Vic Kovacs.
Description: New York : PowerKids Press, 2017. | Series: Ancient cultures and civilizations | Includes index.
Identifiers: ISBN 9781508150077 (pbk.) | ISBN 9781508150022 (library bound) | ISBN 9781508149934 (6 pack)
Subjects: LCSH: Mongols--History--Juvenile literature. | Mongols--Social life and customs--Juvenile literature.
Classification: LCC GN548.K68 2017 | DDC 951'.7--dc23

Developed and produced for Rosen by BlueAppleWorks Inc.

Art Director: Haley Harasymiw
Managing Editor for BlueAppleWorks: Melissa McClellan
Editors: Janice Dyer, Marcia Abramson
Design: T.J. Choleva

Picture credits: p. 5, 8 Picturehouse/Photofest; p. 7 Public Domain; p. 11, 12 left, 12 U. S. Marine Corps/Sgt. G. S. Thomas/Public Domain; p. 11 inset Creative Commons; p. 13 Bill Taroli/Creative Commons; p. 15 inset Sergei Vasilyevich Ivanov/Public Domain; p. 15 Артур Орльонов/Creative Commons; p. 16 inset Edwin Lord Weeks/Public Domain; p. 16 Leopold Müller/Public Domain; p. 19 Rawpixel.com/Shutterstock; p. 20 Anige/Public Domain; p. 23 inset Maxim Petrichuk/Shutterstock; p. 23 Alex Brylov/Shutterstock; p. 24 left Dmitry Chulov/Shutterstock; p. 24 JingAiping/Shutterstock; p. 25 inset, 25 TTstudio/Shutterstock; p. 27 Andrey Burmakin/Shutterstock; p. 27 inset hecke61/Shutterstock; p. 29 inset U.S. Army National Guard photo by Sgt. Marisa Lindsay/Released/Public Domain; p. 29 Vidor/Public Domain; Maps: p. 14 T.J. Choleva; p. 28 T.J. Choleva

Manufactured in the United States of America
CPSIA Compliance Information: Batch #BS16PK: For Further Information contact Rosen Publishing, New York, New York at 1-800-237-9932

CONTENTS

CHAPTER 1

WARRIORS OF ASIAN STEPPES

The area called the Mongolian **Plateau** has been **inhabited** for thousands of years. It is located in central Asia. The area is also called the Mongolian **steppe**. A steppe is a large, flat area of land with few trees and lots of grass. The Mongolian steppe is surrounded by the Altai Mountains in the west, the Gobi Desert in the south, and Siberia in the north. These natural barriers kept out invaders, but they also restricted the number of people who migrated to the area. The people who lived there all shared the same language and way of life.

Most people living there practiced a **nomadic** lifestyle. This meant that they didn't have permanent homes, and were constantly moving around the country. They lived in **clans**, which were made up of different families. These clans would travel around the country, hunting and tending **livestock**. These clans were part of larger groups called tribes. Members of the tribes were all related to a common **ancestor**. These tribes often fought against each other for a variety of reasons.

In the early 1100s, a group of Mongol tribes came together to form the Khamag Mongol confederation. Its first leader, Kabul Khan, fought successfully against invasions of the Jin Dynasty of China. The **alliance** was quite powerful until the end of the twelfth century, when the confederation began to weaken.

Mongolia is the original homeland of both Turks and Mongols. The history for these two groups is closely related, and their languages are similar.

CHAPTER 2

GENGHIS KHAN

The Khamag Mongol confederation rule was limited to the Mongolian Plateau area. It took the military genius of a powerful Mongol leader to unite the Khamag Mongol and other clans and to bring about the sudden expansion of the Mongols from their homeland in the thirteenth century. He was born with the name of Temujin, but became known to all as Genghis Khan.

During the early thirteenth century, northeast Asia was divided into several tribes and confederations, including Naimans, Merkits, Tatars, Khamag Mongols, and Khereids. Each tribe was powerful in their own right and often unfriendly toward each other, raiding and looting their neighbors.

The one warrior to unite them all one day, Temujin, was born around 1162. He was a descendant of Kabul Khan through his father's family. Kabul Khan was his great-grandfather.

SECRETS OF GENGHIS KHAN

Genghis Khan never let anyone paint his **portrait** while he was alive. As a result, no one really knows what he truly looked like. Later paintings and drawings are just guesses. Descriptions of him while he was alive claim that he had cat-like eyes, long hair, and a long beard.

Genghis Khan's grandson, Kublai Khan, had a portrait of Genghis Khan painted almost 50 years after his death. It is the only portrait of the leader that still exists today. Kublai Khan asked some of Genghis Khan's warriors to make sure the portrait was accurate.

When Temujin was only nine, his father was killed by a rival Tatar tribe. Young Temujin declared himself the chief of the clan, but the clan refused to be led by such a young child. Temujin and his family were banished and struggled to survive for the next several years. Young Temujin was even a slave for a time, but he escaped.

Shortly afterward, he met up with his brothers and other members of his clan and formed a fighting band. This band would soon grow to an army of 20,000 men. His mother, Hoelun, had taught him the importance of forming alliances between tribes while he was growing up. With his army, Temujin set out to form one alliance with all tribes, with him as their leader.

Genghis Khan's army was made up of skilled archers and horse riders. They were fierce warriors. Genghis Khan used military strength and **diplomacy** to unite the different tribes.

TOMB OF GENGHIS KHAN

Genghis Khan died in 1227 and divided his conquered lands among his sons and grandsons. He had one unusual request after his death: he didn't want anyone to know where he was buried. According to tradition, tribal leaders were buried without markings of any kind. As a result, many legends about his **tomb** have sprung up. One claims that the procession bringing his body back to Mongolia killed anyone they met, to keep their path secret. After the tomb was built, it's believed the slaves who constructed it were killed by soldiers, who were then killed themselves. One location where he may have been buried is the Khentii Province, near where he was born. Wherever it is, it's claimed that various efforts were made to hide it, like diverting a river over the site. Others say trees were planted on top of it, or many horses were ridden over it. Today, the location of the tomb is still unknown. Exactly how Genghis Khan died is also a mystery.

One of his first orders of business was to **avenge** his father's death by destroying the Tatar army. Next, Temujin's Mongols defeated the Taichi'ut. Merkits were also defeated and forced under Temujin's rule. By 1206, Temujin had defeated the powerful Naiman tribe, which gave him control of central and eastern Mongolia.

Seeing his victories, other tribes took peace when it was offered. This was considered a better option than having to fight such a merciless opponent. Temujin was named the "Genghis Khan," or universal leader of the Mongols. Now the leader of a vast fighting force, Khan quickly began conquering new territory. By the time he died in 1227, he had started forming what would one day become one of the largest empires history would ever know.

CHAPTER 3

THE MONGOL EMPIRE

Today, the Mongol army is mostly remembered for its brutality. If a city did not surrender to the Mongols, it would be destroyed and most of its people killed. However, if it did surrender, it was treated with a surprising level of tolerance. People living in the empire were allowed to continue practicing their own religions. As a result, the empire came to have Christians, Buddhists, Muslims, and more. It also improved **infrastructure**, building roads and other projects. The famous Silk Road, a network of trading routes throughout Asia and into Europe, came under sole control of the Mongol Empire. An early kind of postal service was even set up using these roads!

THE INVINCIBLE MONGOL ARMY

There were many reasons the Mongol army was one of the best in history. Genghis Khan reorganized his army to break down the **traditional** clan-based divisions that had previously caused conflict among Mongols. He introduced a system of **meritocracy**. This system meant that people were promoted to better positions based on their skills rather than their family's power. This was very different from the system that was in place before Genghis Khan came to power.

Genghis Khan's army relied on a breed of horse called Mongol horses. They were excellent warhorses because of their incredible endurance. All Mongol riders used stirrups, which made riding and fighting on horses much easier.

Under the old system, leaders inherited their positions through family and clan connections, although they often did not have the necessary leadership skills. Under the new meritocratic system, people who had proven themselves worthy of leadership were put in charge. There were different ways to prove one was worthy, such as showing bravery during battle.

The army itself was arranged based on a decimal system. This meant that all units were based on multiples of ten. These included the smallest, the arban, which had ten members. The members of an arban were expected to be loyal to one another and to their commanders, regardless of their clan or ethnic origin. Next came the zuun, which was made up of ten arbans, or one hundred men. Then came the myangan, made up of ten zuuns, or one thousand men. Lastly was the tumen, which was made up of ten myangans, or ten thousand men.

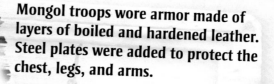

Mongol troops wore armor made of layers of boiled and hardened leather. Steel plates were added to protect the chest, legs, and arms.

When the Mongol warriors encountered walled cities, they quickly learned to **besiege** them.

Most Mongol troops were light **cavalry**, using bows and arrows to attack from a distance. The rest were heavier hitters, and used **lances** for closer combat. Mongol soldiers were expert horsemen. They were trained to serve together as a cavalry force, or individually as scouts. Each man usually had at least two horses, and some had as many as four. This allowed them to change horses often, so they could quickly cover huge distances.

Mongol forces were very good at using **psychological warfare** to help them win battles. Towns were generally given a chance to surrender. If they did, they were mostly allowed to continue as before, but paid tribute to the Mongol Empire. If they didn't, the town was destroyed, and almost everyone in it killed. The few survivors were then sent out to tell the story of their town's destruction. The Mongols hoped that other towns would surrender out of terror once they heard of the army's ferocity.

CONQUERING ALL

After uniting the tribes of his homeland, Genghis Khan soon set his sights on the rest of Asia. In 1210 he conquered Western Xia, located in what is today known as northwestern China. He then declared war on the Jin Dynasty, at the time the ruling power of northern China. The Mongols took the Jin capital Yanjing (called Beijing today) in 1215, though the Jin Dynasty would hold on until 1234.

Perhaps his most impressive campaign was against the Muslim Khwarezm Empire that ruled parts of Persia and Afghanistan. Genghis Khan reached out to the Khwarezm peacefully at first by sending a caravan of traders to negotiate trade agreements. When he learned that the diplomatic party was arrested by one of the Khwarezm governors, Genghis Khan sent three diplomats to the ruler of the Khwarezm

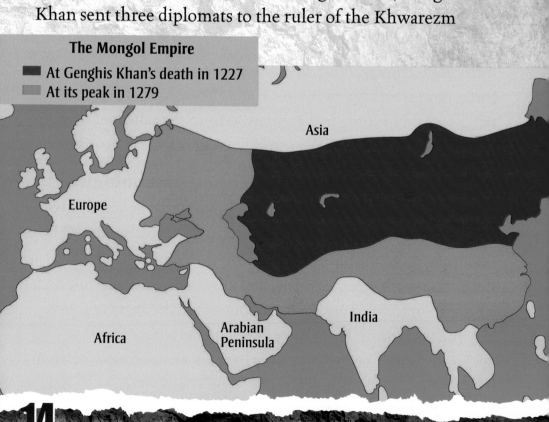

The Mongol Empire
- At Genghis Khan's death in 1227
- At its peak in 1279

Asia

Europe

Africa

Arabian
Peninsula

India

By 1240, Mongol troops had conquered most of Russia. Then, the armies continued on to invade Poland and Hungary in 1241.

Empire, Shah Muhammed, with demands that the governor be sent to him for punishment. The shah refused and sent back the severed head of one of the diplomats instead. This would prove to be a fatal mistake. Filled with rage by the repeated insults, Genghis Khan attacked the empire. The war lasted less than two years. In the years of 1219 to 1221, the Khwarezm Empire was completely destroyed.

Although Genghis Khan died in 1227, his empire's dreams of conquest would not. His descendants continued to spread Mongol rule after his death. In Europe, Russia saw many Mongol invasions, with both Moscow and Kiev falling between 1238 and 1240. Modern Iraq, Iran, Syria, and other parts of western Asia were also conquered by Mongols.

They won the siege of Baghdad in 1258, and looted the city that had been the seat of Islamic power in the world for five centuries. Japan managed to avoid being taken, but Korea and much of southern Asia were not so lucky. Genghis's grandson, Kublai Khan, even became the ruler of China, and the first emperor of the Yuan Dynasty.

PAX MONGOLICA

The more territory the Mongol Empire acquired, the more stable life became for the people living in it. This was because, for the first time ever, many different areas were under the control of a single empire and its laws. This new order has become known as **Pax** Mongolica.

The huge Mongol empire stretched from China and southern parts of Asia all the way to Eastern Europe, joining the eastern and western world together. One of the main

During the Pax Mongolica, trade routes became safe for travel. Trade grew as caravans of traders from many countries traveled across the empire to sell their goods.

MONGOL LAWS AND RULES

Genghis Khan created a code of law called Yassa. The Yassa included laws for soldiers, officers, and doctors, as well as others. The laws focused on three things: obedience to Genghis Khan, ensuring connections between the nomad clans, and punishment of those who disobeyed. It acted as the law of the land in the Mongol Empire. Much of it was created to reduce fighting between clans and tribes and to protect trade. For example, blood feuds were outlawed, and so was theft. Yassa also guaranteed religious freedom throughout the empire, ordering that equal respect and treatment be given to all religions. The penalty for breaking the law could be severe. The most common punishment was death by beheading.

ways this was accomplished was by making trade routes, such as the Silk Road, safer. Merchants could then bring goods from one end of the empire to the other. This allowed them to share not just products and information, but also their cultures.

This period of peace brought many things to new parts of the world. For instance, paper and printing processes from China spread all the way to Europe. Gunpowder was another popular Chinese export at this time. Bills of exchange also began to become popular. These were a kind of paper money similar to what we use today. They freed merchants from having to carry heavy metal coins for an entire journey and made trading easier. Another important innovation introduced was the Yam, an early kind of postal service. Relay stations were built about 30 miles (48 km) apart. It took about a day for messengers on horseback to ride from one station to the next, where they got fresh horses for the next stage. This allowed communication between the east and the west to expand.

CHAPTER 4

MONGOL WAY OF LIFE

Genghis Khan gave his family members and loyal soldiers large pieces of land as rewards for their service. Every time the Mongol army conquered another region, members of the royal family, nobles, warriors, as well as deserving servants, each received their share of the goods seized.

Even though the Mongol Empire was made up of various ethnic and religious groups and tribes, Genghis Khan insisted that all loyalty was focused only on him. He did not tolerate divisions between clans, and expected obedience from everyone. Life in the Mongol Empire was based on obeying laws and discipline. The empire was considered to be very safe and well-run. Theft and destruction of property were strictly forbidden. Genghis Khan valued freedom of religion, and virtually every religion was represented in the Mongol Empire. Religious leaders did not have to pay taxes during his rule. His son built a number of places of worship in the capital city for Buddhist, Muslim, Christian, and Taoist believers.

The empire was ruled by a system called kurultai. The system involved a council of chiefs and leaders who got together to discuss and make decisions about the issues of the day. Families voted on an issue by showing up for an event. If a family did not show up, it was considered a vote against the issue.

Armed patrols of Mongol warriors traveled the empire to enforce the Yassa laws. They punished offenders if necessary.

Over time, Mongol rulers adopted some of the local customs of the regions they defeated. Only rulers of steppe heartlands lived the traditional Mongol lifestyle.

A good example was Kublai Khan, Genghis Khan's grandson, who founded the Yuan Dynasty after the Mongol armies conquered China. He knew that ethnic Mongols in his empire were few in number and could not successfully rule the Chinese majority in a Mongol way. Instead, he used Chinese political and cultural ideas and relied on his Chinese advisers. Over time, he became a traditional type of Chinese emperor. He focused his attention on China and mostly ignored his Mongol homeland. However, he maintained Mongol traditions within the walled Forbidden City.

Kublai Khan was the fifth Great Khan of the Mongol Empire. He was the founder of the Yuan Dynasty in China.

THE FORBIDDEN CITY

The Forbidden City is a walled city in modern-day Beijing. It is one of the most famous locations in China, and it is where many Chinese emperors ruled from. However, it was originally built to keep the Chinese culture out! Originally constructed by Kublai Khan, it was meant to be a Mongol sanctuary, where the Khan and other Mongols could keep their culture and way of life alive. The city was filled with gers, the traditional tents of the Mongols. These are where the Khan's wives gave birth, as well as where Mongol children were educated. Though Kublai and later Khans ruled as Chinese emperors, in the Forbidden City, they were still Mongols.

NOMADS OF THE STEPPES

The Mongol people were traditionally nomads. This meant that they didn't have permanent homes, but moved to different areas based on the season and other factors. Even during Genghis Khan's rule, many Mongols lived as herders. However, they were always prepared to go to war when called to arms.

Mongol herders were constantly on the move to new pastures where their animals could graze. The most common kinds of livestock were horses, cows, goats, sheep, and camels. Most animals were milked to make foods such as cheese and yogurt. Their meat also served as food, and their hides were turned into clothing and shelter. The Mongols, and their animals, were well adapted to severe weather conditions on the steppes as well as occasional shortages of food and water.

FAMILY STRUCTURE OF ORDINARY MONGOLS

The traditional Mongol family was **patriarchal**. The father was the head of the family in Mongol society. Marriage was important, with sons having wives brought to them, and daughters being sent to other families as wives. In this way, alliances between clans were made.

Once a son was old enough to be married, he was given a part of his family's herd, as well as a portion of their grazing lands. The older the son, the larger his herd and section of land. Parents were well provided for in their old age. The youngest son was expected to stay with his aging parents in their tent as their caretaker. He would then inherit the tent once they died, along with the rest of their herd.

Boys very early learned three important skills: horse riding, hunting, and herding. These skills allowed them to provide for their families. They also came in handy once they entered the military at the age of fifteen. Girls, on the other hand, were in charge of the home. They took care of domestic chores, such as milking livestock, sewing, and cooking. Taking care of their families was their main goal. They usually also knew how to herd, and loaded up their family **yurt** when it came time to move. Although men held the power in Mongol society, women had more influence than in many other societies. Men often asked their wives for guidance in important matters. Genghis Khan's wife Borte was his trusted adviser.

TIMELESS YURTS

Yurts are still in use today by people in Mongolia, China, and Kyrgyzstan. Of course, modern ones use more modern materials, but much of the design is the same!

Yurts were the ideal homes for nomads. They could easily load the wooden frame and felt covering onto camels or cattle and move them to new locations.

PORTABLE DWELLINGS

Mongols lived in gers, which literally meant "home." They are also known by their Turkish name, yurts. They were round, portable structures. The frames were made of wood, and they were covered in felt. The frames were collapsible, and they could be quickly broken down for moving, usually within an hour. It took about the same amount of time to put them back up. They had pointed roofs, so that rain and snow would run off of them. The point of the roof could be opened to let out smoke, or closed to keep out rain or snow. The fire pit in the center was used to heat the home. They tended to be warm in the winter and cool in the summer, which made them ideal dwellings for all seasons.

HERDING AND HUNTING

Animals played a central role in the lives of Mongolian herders. The most important animal was the horse. Smaller than most, the Mongolian horses were known for being able to travel long distances without getting tired. Important in both family and military life, horses were beloved. Mistreating a horse was even considered a crime, and those who did so could be punished severely.

Sheep and goats were extremely useful animals. They provided milk, wool, and meat, all of which were important to survival on the steppes. Sheep wool was used to make the felt that covered yurts, providing important shelter. Wool was also used to make rugs that covered the dirt floors of their homes, as well as clothing. Cattle and camels were generally used to carry heavy loads, but they also provided milk. Camels were especially valued for their unique wool.

Mongols depended on sheep and goats for food and wool. They had large flocks to provide the wool needed to make their clothing and the thick felt needed to cover their yurts.

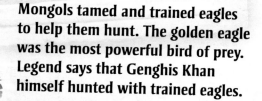

Mongols tamed and trained eagles to help them hunt. The golden eagle was the most powerful bird of prey. Legend says that Genghis Khan himself hunted with trained eagles.

Mongols didn't rely just on their livestock for meat. They were also skilled hunters. Common prey included rabbit, deer, and wild boar. They were even known to eat large rodents such as squirrels and marmots!

For Mongols, food fell into one of two categories: white foods and brown foods. During the summer, they tended to eat mostly white foods. These were usually dairy based, and made from the milk of their livestock. Cheese, yogurt, and airag, fermented milk from a female horse, were common staples of a Mongol diet. Brown foods were mostly meats. These were what Mongols ate during the winter. A common dish was boiled meat with a side of wild garlic. Eating utensils weren't widely used, so everything was basically finger food.

CHAPTER 5

DOWNFALL AND LEGACY

Before he died, Genghis Khan divided his empire among his sons and grandsons. He gave his son Ogedei control of most of eastern Asia, including China. Ogedei became the second Great Khan of the Mongol Empire. He gave his second son, Chagatai, control over central Asia and northern Iran. His youngest son, Tolui, received a small territory near the Mongol homeland. Finally, he gave his grandson, Batu, control over what is now modern Russia.

The Mongol Empire included a massive area of land. As a result, later empires in the region all have their roots in the Mongol Empire. The Moghul Empire of India emerged from Genghis Khan's son Chagatai's rule over central Asia. One of his grandsons, Hulagu Khan, founded the Ilkhanate, which became the heart of Persia. Another grandson, Kublai Khan, unified China. From then on, even though China experienced a number of different dynasties, the country remained unified.

Kublai Khan not only ruled China as their emperor, he also ruled the entire Mongol Empire as Grand Khan. However, his **successors** weren't so lucky. They eventually became seen as too Chinese, and the other Khanates refused to recognize their authority.

A giant sculpture of Genghis Khan stands guard near Mongolia's modern-day capital of Ulaanbaatar. It was built in 2008.

The Yuan Dynasty that Kublai established was overthrown by the Ming Dynasty in 1368. The Yuan leaders fled back to Mongolia, and established the Northern Yuan Dynasty, which lasted until the seventeenth century. Gradually, the other Khanates further west also lost power. Unlike other empires, there wasn't one big event that led to the fall. There was no great battle or last stand that clearly ended the reign of the Mongols. Instead, the various Khanates became more and more isolated, and gradually their power faded. The last Khanate, the Khanate of Kiva, lasted in Russia until 1920.

The end of the Mongol Empire was also the end of a period of great stability throughout Asia. The Silk Road and other trade routes were no longer as safe as they had been. Trade and communications were disrupted at first and eventually taken over by the Muslim Ottoman Empire.

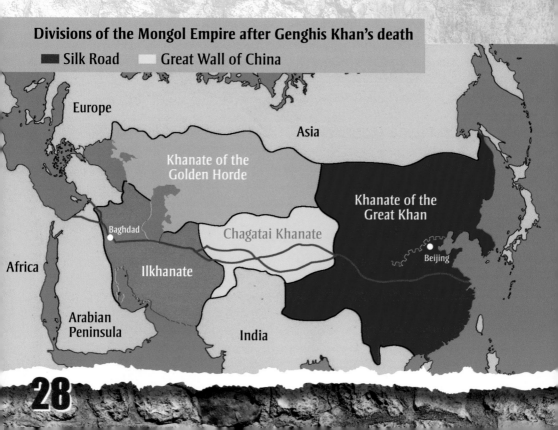

Divisions of the Mongol Empire after Genghis Khan's death
■ Silk Road   □ Great Wall of China

Europe

Asia

Khanate of the Golden Horde

Khanate of the Great Khan

Baghdad

Chagatai Khanate

Beijing

Africa

Ilkhanate

Arabian Peninsula

India

Naadam is the largest festival in modern Mongolia. The participants compete in wrestling, horse racing, and archery. The festival celebrates the traditional Mongolian warrior heritage.

At its height, the Mongol Empire was the largest land-bound empire in history. Some claim the death toll from Mongol wars was as high as 40 million people. Despite the brutality that his army was known for, Genghis Khan was known to rule his people fairly. The uniting of the eastern and western worlds under Mongol law allowed for the trade of information that greatly broadened the horizons of people on both sides.

Modern Mongolia is all that is left from the once mighty Mongol Empire. Mongolians are fully aware of the unique history of their country. Today, Genghis Khan is viewed as a hero, and many Mongolians look back on the accomplishments of the empire proudly.

GLOSSARY

alliance: an agreement between two parties to work together

ancestor: a relative from the past

avenge: to harm or punish someone who has harmed you

besiege: to surround a city or area with soldiers and try to take control of it

cavalry: the part of an army with soldiers who ride horses

clan: a large group of people who are related or who have the same goal

diplomacy: maintaining good relations between different governments

infrastructure: the basic structures needed for a region to function properly, such as roads and bridges

inhabited: lived in

lance: a type of sword

livestock: farm animals

meritocracy: a system where people move ahead based on their talent

nomadic: not living in a fixed place, but moving as needed based on factors such as the weather and animal migrations

patriarchal: headed by a man

pax: Latin for peace

plateau: a large flat area of land

portrait: a picture showing a person

psychological warfare: the use of threats and terror to threaten and scare one's enemy

steppe: a large flat area of land with grass and few trees

successor: someone who follows another person

tomb: a room in which bodies are housed after death

traditional: the way something has often been done in the past

yurt: a round tent made of wood and stretched skins or felt

FOR MORE INFORMATION

Books

Ceceri, Kathy. *The Silk Road: Explore the World's Most Famous Trade Route with 20 Projects.* White River Junction, VT: Nomad Press, 2011.

Krull, Kathleen. *Kubla Khan: The Emperor of Everything.* City, Sate: Viking Books for Young Readers, 2010.

Medina, Nico. *Who Was Genghis Khan?* New York, NY: Grosset & Dunlap, 2014.

Websites

Due to the changing nature of Internet links, PowerKids Press has developed an online list of websites related to the subject of this book. This site is updated regularly. Please use this link to access the list:

www.powerkidslinks.com/acc/mongols

INDEX